Poetic Lifelines

Poetic Lifelines
Volume 1

TANIA R. BRYANT

Charleston, SC

www.PalmettoPublishing.com

Poetic Lifelines: Volume 1

Copyright © 2022 by Tania R. Bryant

All rights reserved

First Edition

Paperback ISBN: 978-1-68515-138-6

Contents

What Lies beyond What We See

In between the cracks

Could be so simple

An infusion of real taste

Is so bittersweet

Magnifying what we see

Realms in factors that can't be seen

Stuck in the abyss

Things we wish to encounter

Sights that are revoked

The feeling as we choke

Sucked in through the blur

Of such that concur

What is in front

What is behind

Lies an obscene thing we see

Behind that lens, we are free

I see you

You see me

A reflection so complex

Underneath the surface

Thoughts are so perplexed

To be defined by what is really next

* * *

This generation that I am so fond to be in takes the easier way out of things. Whatever the case may be involving personal situations, education, love, and life in general. We are a very broad group that does not take the time to recognize and understand our individual drive and potential. We are capable of so much more than we tend to think. It's deeper than deep. We are staring right at it. We tend to maneuver away from the obvious or to lessen our knowledge of what is and what can be. We can go into everything we do and love with so much more. In between those cracks is a road of greatness. The lens is a focal point for our dreams and aspirations. This realization is expressed through the poem above.

Reflection

_____

_____

_____

_____

_____

_____

_____

_____

_____

_____

_____

_____

_____

_____

_____

_____

_____

_____

_____

_____

_____

_____

_____

_____

_____

Beauty That Unfolds

Upon the surface

Holds substance

Highs and lows

Weakest and highest links

The real that is hidden

Behind the walls of a broken lock

Too scared to unveil its purpose

Through the eyes that make up the lock

Awaiting clarity, promise, and love

Shackles waiting to be unshackled

Tears waiting to be wiped

The smile wanting to always appear

Every single thought to be shared with ease

Something simple

Something twisted

Something waiting

It's full of beauty

The beast is unfolding

A beautiful beast indeed

* * *

Beauty is more than an understatement. It's only highly favored when we on a general spectrum talk about attraction or observations that can objectify an individual's body. Their lack of that's not what it is. I promise that is 5 percent of it. That 95 percent resembles how we as people interact, understand ourselves and others—the different attributes that we are driven by, what makes an individual unique. The good, bad, and the ugly. That is all beauty is seen to be. Your beauty is discovered through your own light, the experiences you have, and the environment you are surrounded by. Through these lenses I have developed a poem as such.

Reflection

Silence

4 walls

Completely surrounded

Mind

Is clouded

Air

Is dry

The quiet

Is near

The feeling of emptiness

Is displayed

Consumed by nothingness

* * *

I picture myself in whatever environment I am most at ease. I believe we call it a daydream or zoning out. The world stops for seconds to minutes. It's just me, myself, and I. Within that time, I have experienced silence more than ever before. It is an intangible feeling or…not. Mmm.

Reflection

One Mind, Two Souls

There was one

Then became two

Hand in hand

Heart for heart

Love

Lust not found

Something real

Forever intertwined

Through the eyes

Of two souls

Brings a story

To life

A fantasy

A fiction

Brought upon two beings

Where you do not question what's real

* * *

The place of comfort and safeness. The two close-knit expressions can be so pure between two beings that have utmost love for each other. It's a soul tie that not only brings two together from within but also means one cannot function without the other. It's a story that is an aspiring experience every individual longs to have.

Reflection

SOUL FOOD

Richness of the heart

Lays out love, laughter, and liveliness

Among the people we love

Expressed through the food we make

This is what we are made of

Lingering smells, sensational sounds of voices

The heart of coming together, soft-spoken words

Outgoing upbringings of trials & triumph

Unforgettable tragic, loving memories

Faith that should never be given up on

Opening of your heart…Ongoing aspirations

Divinity of true happiness

Everything that is sought upon

Food…love…people…family…life…

Is all here within the palms of your hands

Grasp all of it, embrace it…your SOUL FOOD

* * *

This poem spoke to me the most because I value family strongly. It's a lens in the light of what family means to me, how memorably each transition of my life until right now has really made me value how I was brought up, the various family members I've had unforgettable conversations with, and even the worst moments ever that I have experienced. It's really a cry of joy of how blessed I am to have a beautiful family. Family can be quite daunting, but I promise you it's so precious.

Reflection

You

I observe

What do you see?

I read

What do you hear?

I listen

What do you comprehend?

I understand

Can you see between the lines?

I kiss

Do you feel my touch?

I touch

How does it feel?

Soft wet sensation I feel upon ya lips

Shrivels me up inside

The vibrations of your body

Follow the rhythm of your breath

Can you feel it?

Inhale and exhale

Slow and steady

As you come to a peak

High as what u can control

Leaving nothing but a sensation

Something I feel

Something I see

Something you want

grab

moan

go

Until you can't anymore

lick

bite

Do you want it?

touch

hold your breath

mind is squirming

Is it okay?

Sure it is

You like it

I love it

No

I like it

You love it

As it should be

* * *

This is a very intense poem that not only articulates sexual persuasion but can also be quite stimulating to the mind. Food for thought! It's about the ability to be a pleasure to someone very special or who you may be attractive to—even yet providing a safeness where guidance and patience with an individual can be very sexy. Why not just see something for just what it is? To be sensual in all rhythms, understanding someone's mind and body, is a rare intimacy. I'm sure reading left a very explicit scenery in your head with mind-boggling thoughts. It is a natural thing to experience. Enjoy!

Reflection

_____
_____
_____
_____
_____
_____
_____
_____
_____
_____
_____
_____
_____
_____
_____
_____
_____
_____
_____
_____
_____
_____
_____
_____
_____
_____

Black Lives Matter

The words that spark news
Taken back by derogatory slurs from a few
What Is and What Was known as history
Has carried on through a blind view
What was…
The white separated from the black
Laws that prohibited equality
Disgraceful gestures and threats toward families
Destruction of infrastructure through hatred
Drivenness to scorch the hearts and lives of innocent beings
The history that has impacted this world is set in stone
History is inevitable to forget but reaps the truth
Of what was and what is now
Now…
Racial profiling
Minority undermining
Police officers conniving
Press constantly misinterpreting
What is the reasoning
Is the time we have worth teaching, expressing, and fighting
Black matters, white matters, all matter
If that is the case
What is with the…

Objectifying

Patronizing

Traumatizing

I promise the love is wanted for everyone and everywhere

This world makes it hard to want to replenish and make change of what
has been recycling for years

What has been tried

What has been fought for

The feeling of being suffocated by what we should be protected by

The biases that conflict with our judgment of what is to be true or false

What has to be done

What really has to be changed

We are alone

We are together

No one sees our pain

No one understands this history

Our history that strikes the white man

Through the madness we still rise

We rise in voice

We rise in strength

We rise in salvation

What once tried to be hidden

Has always been here and found

Open your eyes

We are here and you have no choice but to see

* * *

A very difficult topic. Many others may feel a lot of rage from many eye-opening events that have happen in the era of slavery, in the civil rights movement, and even in today's society. It breaks me down in many ways to notice many derogatory actions and slurs that have been done, heard, and seen, whether in my life personally, toward a family member or friends, or just in the media. This topic deserved an expression of how I have known it to be and what is in the works of change that has been happening.

Reflection

_____
_____
_____
_____
_____
_____
_____
_____
_____
_____
_____
_____
_____
_____
_____
_____
_____
_____
_____
_____
_____
_____
_____
_____

The Possibility between You & Me

Time with me shall not be forced

The easiness of letting it play its course

It's quite simple but leaves trails of curiosity

Every minute, day, and hour

Something so small could be so loud and meaningful

The time that is shared between two of a kind

Keep in mind, there are possibilities of the divine

It's sickening but bearable to believe

You and I are something that can be so pristine

As pure as water that drops on a blooming flower

Looking into my eyes glimmers sweet and sour

It's not perfect but it's just right

Through this disguise that we call life

Buckle in, watch me take you on this flight

As the comfort in this space that could be shared

All the hatred and disappointment that breathe down your neck
will disappear

Positivity and love that scorch through the air

Grab you afloat of such love upon my frontier

The high chances of you seeking me

Will lay out the blueprint of what should have always been

If a calling is so destined to aspire

Look at me and tell me what impeccable wishes you desire

The chances await

The decisions may contemplate

Rather time should stop or wait

Being in the midst of this existence

Makes love a special fate

The expectations may be high

So let me just clarify

The real who provide themselves in every way

Will make a real one want to stay

The complications brought in today's society

Break down our emotional, mental, and physical being

Embrace what is real

Embrace what is true

Embrace all the possibilities

What is real in me and what is real in you

Defines us deeply and I must say it's true

What is brought to the table is our key to our heart

How we express this key and how we carry this key

Forsakes any negative being that comes its way

This key is special

This key is beautiful

This key opens doors

This key opens walls that are forbidden

This key will never strike the wrong cloth

This key is me awaiting a possibility

That the key to you and me marks an openness of inseparable capabilities

Of holding one's trust

Of believing in one's care
Of understanding one's flaws
This possibility is quite clear
That something in the future is near
You and me
I see that possibility there

* * *

The outer and inner layers of Tania Raquel Bryant. Of course I am not perfect, but I believe that everyone deserves a poem about what things could possibly be like—knowing me as a human being and the layers of my faults, beauty, personality, and how such can be channeled through society. It's not so clear per se, but that is why there is the possibility of experiencing an understanding of who I am and how I see things through my lens.

Reflection

_____
_____
_____
_____
_____
_____
_____
_____
_____
_____
_____
_____
_____
_____
_____
_____
_____
_____
_____
_____
_____
_____
_____
_____
_____
_____

The Truth

This arose

The feelings were as simple as could be

No thought of another

In the moment where we stood

Strings were definitely attached

No one could say anything

It was just us, only us

Hidden behind the truth lay caution

What was real had to open the gates in our reality

What was left back home

Never went away

The thoughts were scarce because all I had was you

All I wanted was you

maybe you more than I

Emotions

Variations

Touchings

All in one came upon the surface

Never wanting to be forgotten

Locked within our hearts

Separation definitely hit us with no questions

Realizing the truth was not so real

There was an understanding

We can only see us being more than

Being less than was not in question

Tied up, wanting to be released

From the truth was I was not living

Experiencing with someone else

You

There were tears

Quiet closet sits

No responses

Understanding what was wanted could not be acknowledged then

Both knew the sorrow in what we call

Leaving

Dull in moment of denial

The main thing that was not intended to happen

Further in time

Emotions hold on strong

More than expected while yours slows swaying

Away with no guard of what was

But then and now

Looking back, it's beyond hard

Crushing

But is it worth the fight?

Time-consuming

The time I wish I had

To fix

To create

To understand

Why

This was not the time

Was not my time

This is the truth

* * *

The truth about anything we may seem to avoid. First, because it could be some sort of rejection. Second, because it may cause you to see something you did not realize about yourself. Third is the power that truth can hold over a person. It's definitely an assurance that could be best for you or be a rude awakening to something bad. That can be a judgment call. Truth is an understanding that may lead to curious thoughts when it comes to love, death, and money. I laid my words out with confessions, lessons learned, and an open mind going forward into my future. The truth will set you free.

Reflection

_____

_____

_____

_____

_____

_____

_____

_____

_____

_____

_____

_____

_____

_____

_____

_____

_____

_____

_____

_____

_____

_____

_____

_____

_____

Dreams

The mind that feeds

During the realm of a deep sleep

It remembers

It forgets

The attachment can be so senile

Flashbacks of denial

Beautiful moments as such make us smile

Was it real, is it real, will it become real?

The mind that is working

Continuously moving the motions of how we feel

Could it be real?

The baggage of what eats away at us

The slight exposure of hate, love, and depression

All in one captures light flashing upon our eyes

In the midst of REM where no control compels

Needless to say, what we cherish may prevail

The mind that wonders

Makes thoughts a reality

Deaths a mortality

Family much of a camaraderie

Hookups blindly a fantasy

Fuckups expressed through insanity

We control what we can't control

So sublime from what is true and what lies

Such a disguise of what we want to deny

Kid me from a fool but this message implies

What's in state of mind

The mind that seeks

The mind that competes

The mind that loves

The mind that deviates

The mind that endures in rooms of openness

Holds a sense of supreme

Open your eyes

It's just a dream

* * *

I'm sure everyone has experienced a dream. Whether it makes you wake up in the middle of the night, whole body sweating, or even just realize your sheets are wet from a wet dream. They can vary from real lifetime events or memories to fantasy scenes of particular individuals or something of your interest. It's a stimulation in all, no matter what it can be. It's something crazy if remembered vs. not even being able to figure it out at times. What may cause you to dream? Would you rather remember your dreams or not?

Reflection

_____

_____

_____

_____

_____

_____

_____

_____

_____

_____

_____

_____

_____

_____

_____

_____

_____

_____

_____

_____

_____

Loyalty

What do we all stand for?

The truth more or what lies in between the cracks

What is bounded in one can't be folded

The blood that runs trickles

Holding on by the breath of life

The importance shared among the chosen

It's what we live for

It's what we laugh for

It's what we cry for

Something so rare

Something so precious

Something so sincere

Promises are kept

Decisions are supported

Realization of what's real is not unrecognized

Everything is valued to a T

The special in this cannot be undone

It's sealed from the bottom of the heart

To the blessing of the soul

Once entwined it cannot be drawn apart

It is a hell of a ride

It has finished but again it is just the start

* * *

Loyalty is not just a word you can flash and canter around to anyone you meet. It's a buildup of trust that then interconnects with family. It runs deep and is not a bond that could be easily taken for granted. Cherish what you have with an individual that goes deeper than a friendship or even a relationship.

Reflection

_____
_____
_____
_____
_____
_____
_____
_____
_____
_____
_____
_____
_____
_____
_____
_____
_____
_____
_____
_____
_____
_____
_____
_____
_____

Melanin

God's grace from above

Seeks beauty so perfect

Imperfection at its finest

Overrules disgust from the lowest

Who can't breathe this?

Who can't soak in this?

Who can't work in this?

From the title that is framed

Black kings and queens shall not be ashamed

Embrace all the shades imprinted

The hatred must be forsaken

The skin that is worn

Rightfully given

Honestly wanted

It's sexy

It's breathtaking

It's power that cannot be taken

Secured safely within our hearts

Wishing to be portrayed in the arts

Marks through a whole-hearted scripture

That we present daily through society's picture

* * *

I'm not sure about y'all, but I embrace my skin. Of course it's the pigment that may tell the difference of an individual due to genetics, ethnicity, and even experiments. It's a soul factor of who you are, what you were blessed and born to have. Wear it and live in it. Your confidence lives through you, even more with a glow of melanin. The perfections and imperfections of the skin bring so much power and beauty to the individual. "Melanin" is a poem that opens those barriers that individuals tend to keep closed.

Reflection

_____
_____
_____
_____
_____
_____
_____
_____
_____
_____
_____
_____
_____
_____
_____
_____
_____
_____
_____
_____
_____
_____

Meaning of Life

The overflowing of blessings

Ability to wake

Possibility to take

Fear that we mistake

True reasoning of why we are here

Fulfilling what our ancestors could not

An abundance of what was fought

Way back when

Far back then

There Adam and Eve

The exposure of evil

Proposes the density in life

The shadows that have spoken

Clutter the bad in a mixture of good

The cloud of judgment has woken

We exist in a fine divine

So pure but bittersweet

Overall, there is a heaven that we seek

In life as beautiful as prone to be

Lies a deeper feeling that we shed to speak

* * *

This poem dives into the unexpected. That is the life we all live and take so daringly, not knowing when and the how. It's very frightening, but it is a thing that we do know will happen. Be adamant about living the life you want by any means, of course legally. By all means be happy and free in your own right. Time is always running, so do your best not to waste any. This life shall end when that time comes around, but till then, live it to your utmost ability.

Reflection

_____

_____

_____

_____

_____

_____

_____

_____

_____

_____

_____

_____

_____

_____

_____

_____

_____

_____

_____

_____

_____

_____

_____

_____

_____

A Color

Casts a spell

Expresses a mood

A feeling that propels

Through the eyes

Of your disguise

Story that tells

Of its persona

The soul

That may fold

Behold

Shouts out

Screams loud

Discovers

Uncovers

Who you are

How you are

What you are

Your sign

That aligns

With any other

It's such

A color

* * *

Colors can express people's moods. They can describe an individual. They make darkness feel quite scary. They lighten up a room and complement the skin. They speak to power, meaning, and art. One little color is not so little but speaks so much volume in many things. It's a work of art through the life we live and the society we are a part of.

Reflection

_____

_____

_____

_____

_____

_____

_____

_____

_____

_____

_____

_____

_____

_____

_____

_____

_____

_____

_____

_____

_____

_____

_____

YOLO

The grasp of a hand

Waving in the wind

Believe in where you stand

The distance between you and time

How surreal to be devastated

Things come things go

Overthinking comes into play forsho

Embrace what is here

Love who is near

Enjoy what is done

Establish longline security

To put at ease that insanity

Breathe in the air

Only of which we fear

Conquer your quests

Invited unwanted guests

Time shall be gone and pass

Live it up to the fullest

Your soul will be at peace

Be happy

Live freely

It is not a test

You're destined to live

May the heavens be with you on God's given quest

* * *

"Carpe diem" definitely can resonate with this poem. Take the risk. Go to your dream place. Talk to the individual you have always had your eye on. Eat your favorite foods. Do what you love. Experience what you want. Be who you want to be. This lifetime happens once—until the next lifetime you will be a part of. Own it and live it!

Reflection

_____
_____
_____
_____
_____
_____
_____
_____
_____
_____
_____
_____
_____
_____
_____
_____
_____
_____
_____
_____
_____
_____
_____
_____

Being Broke

Saturated stress

Unwanted press

Thrown right in your face

Looked upon as a disgrace

A drug that has run its course

Forever stuck in a position

In place of given force

The feeling is numb

Unable to continue forward

Five steps right

Ten steps left

A trap of misconception

Reveals life of suck destruction

Your purpose is defined

Not by being broke

But the light you shed of being woke

Dragged into a slumped statue

Lacking future virtue

* * *

This can be a stigma that can either break you or make you into a person who can face barriers in life. It happens to the best of us. At some point in our lives so far it has taken hold of us. The feeling of being broke can be hopeless. It's a sickening feeling. We always seem to make it to the other side. Sometimes being in the dumps is necessary so we can realize something about ourselves. Life is not easy—it's a big-ass roller coaster that can literally be a smack in the face. Being broke is a disadvantage that can lead to something greater. You decide how that comes out to be.

Reflection

_____

_____

_____

_____

_____

_____

_____

_____

_____

_____

_____

_____

_____

_____

_____

_____

_____

_____

_____

_____

_____

_____

_____

_____

_____

_____

_____

Sleepless Nights

The tossing and the turning

Needless to say, I'm yearning

In the countless minutes that feel like hours

Fighting demons that I wish I didn't encounter

The place where your body should be at rest

But really these few nights got me feeling depressed

Something so right just has not felt quite

Watch, on this night I take you on a flight

The mind is going through some turbulence

Moving left, moving right, getting up, lying down

The hectic movements got my body ready to shut down

Something is keeping me from crashing

A sleepless night is the nightmare from a dream

This has been a new certainty of some fashion

Let's not consume the rights that have been spoken

Because right now I have woken

In such a place so dark and quiet

As the clock ticks, my timing is shortening

This sleepless night could be a rude awakening

Imagine this

You're fast asleep in your own peace

As I'm up writing something so obsolete that it

unfortunately could disturb the peace

*** * ***

Some nights the body can't seem to be at rest. The mind seems to skip over rest mode and tends to keep thinking. The body sweats, and various movements are made through the night. This poem came about in the midst of exactly this. Literally everything came within seconds. It was one of those nights where you have a hard time sleeping. To relax I have written this poem. I promise you I slept just like a baby after finishing.

Reflection

_____

_____

_____

_____

_____

_____

_____

_____

_____

_____

_____

_____

_____

_____

_____

_____

_____

_____

_____

_____

_____

_____

_____

Fury Subliminal

As I stand here

Devoting the emotions from within

A clash of titans

Full of wrath and rage

At once gathered on this path

Faced battling a dead end

Smothered by snakes

Two-faced creatures playing the game pretend

It does not add up

The props or the costumes

Intelligent words or disgusting fumes

A disfigured sight

Wondering if I shall play along

Patiently wanting to release a pure light

Calm and collective

Furiously a problem when taunted on

Once observed with precision

Leads me to one decision

One act by one

Repeats

Controls

Deceives

Allows to separate

What's unwanted

Not needed

Falsely represented

It opens

Your subliminal

* * *

You ever realize that an individual tends to get you there—to a place that you never would want to go, another side of you that can be so detrimental to them and to yourself? All you feel is rage, so you tend to fight your mature side that is willing to make something of what is shown and resolve it in a positive manner. Fighting demons may have another meaning. For this poem "fighting demons" indicates dealing with yourself and the negative insights you may hold that can make people's feelings get hurt. It's a test to see who you really are. All along there is control as well that comes into play and forbids you to take that wrong turn. A play with fire and a play on words—it's all a mind game that in the end you win the smart way.

Reflection

_____
_____
_____
_____
_____
_____
_____
_____
_____
_____
_____
_____
_____
_____
_____
_____
_____
_____
_____
_____
_____
_____
_____
_____
_____
_____

So Far Gone

Where do we go from here?
I'm here and you're there
Is it the distance that crosses the line
Something that's really divine?
I question if this was just a waste of time
My heart feels and lingers
Something so precious crumpling in my fingers
I worry
I doubt
I hesitate
To understand what is real amid the unknown
It could be nothing
Just tell me
Friends it is
Where we must stand at this point
This is not what I want but may be what u want
You tell me
A day has gone by where I haven't forgotten u
I call, I text, I try
Something does not sit well
I just know and you can't play me for a fool
Fool
The fool I am, right
The curiosity eats away at my thoughts
Of you, why u don't respond
Why you disregard the communication

I see it

U do it

But that is just who you are

I know you

Or at least I thought I did

I am here

I want to be here

But the signs want me to relocate to someone else's heart

Is that too enduring for you?

Who knows?

I'm sure you don't

I could be doing too much

I think a lot

I love a lot

I joke a lot

That's who I am and who I will always be

What about me or what I've been doing stops the love u have for me

Let me know

I do love you genuinely

The pieces to the puzzle are a blur

Chess is not my forte

Run up the pieces to complete our differences

Let it sink in

I will grant your wishes

So be it

U don't see me

Us

Anything

I will grant your wish

Trust and believe

It will hurt

I will hurt

But if this has to be it

Then it shall

I'll grant your wish

Love

I love you

To what

It is

It shall

It will be

My love

No love

Lost

Till we

Meet again

* * *

There are times where you face conflict, misunderstanding, or even something you do not wish to face. In your eyes it could be dreadful, but on another note it could be opening your heart to a new beginning. It may seem so simple to recognize what may be good for you and what is not. But who is to say it? It's a question that may not be valued enough to provide a response. It's just a trend of thought that can open up different scenarios and ways to overcome certain situations. This is not a reflection of the other individual but a reflection of myself—in the eyes of doubt, curiosity, being content, and being true to self. These all are linings in this given poem. What do you see?

Reflection

Duty

What's that twenty-four thing

The aye sir aye ma'am

Words spoken verbatim

Built like a statue

Protecting the lives at stake

Timeless hours keeping awake

It must really suck

Kept up well in the dumps

Reminding of being back in the slums

This is done in an orderly fashion

By God's given grace

Praying to finally get off duty

Man, can't wait to leave this place

As time is turning

For the dim lights to hit morning

As we present our case

Staring them shinies in the face

Haven't you heard?

The building is well secured

The will and intelligence

To serve with diligence

Align the tasks

Of being on duty

* * *

The experience of being a marine is that we have to stand duty. I'm not quite sure about the other branches. In my case there is something called twenty-four-hour duty. Where I am stationed, my unit does not go by that. Even though I have not fully experienced a twenty-four-hour duty, I have friends who have done it and explained it to me. I even have been on the phone with a friend who was on one. So I'd say I have a good idea of it. It's something I do want to do, but until then this poem is my interpretation of it.

Reflection

Confliction

Open mind of suspicion

Tubes tied with precision

A clash of kin

The turmoil built within

Black and white

Flashing with depth of motion

Misguided through notion

The issue very misconstrued

The middleman can't interfere with this fuel

So problematic but very brand new

Compose the art of this affliction

Rise above a pure confliction

An eye for an eye

The divine in the sky

The mind that rewinds

Forebodes to reconcile the odds

Of such ache

Much to risk and much at stake

What conflicts must shed and wake

* * *

This poem arose from me watching the movie *Love Jones*. It's a romantic movie with the main characters played by the finest Nia Long and Larenz Tate. It portrays the love that they shared, how it all came about, and the troubles that they went through. It's a beautiful movie that shows how deep love can be. Confliction is quite a twist, such as the twist between the lives of a photographer and a poet. If you have not seen this movie, I highly recommend it.

Reflection

_____

_____

_____

_____

_____

_____

_____

_____

_____

_____

_____

_____

_____

_____

_____

_____

_____

_____

_____

_____

_____

_____

Still

No movement

Mild breathing

Air swaying

Tunes fuming

A stillness

Fathom of sound

Movement not found

Still

Silence

Constant surroundings

Overclouded stillness

A feeling not felt

Nothing that is something

It is still

* * *

What can you imagine to be still? Is it tangible or intangible? Does it speak or does it move? When you read this, what is still? Is it the mind? Is it the thoughts that ramble in your head? Is it objects around you that have no sudden movement? What is it?

Reflection

_____

_____

_____

_____

_____

_____

_____

_____

_____

_____

_____

_____

_____

_____

_____

_____

_____

_____

_____

Black Women

Nonetheless a flower

Full of color

Petals of sorrow

Petals of sin

Petals of priorities

Petals that represent a soul factor

An openness of varieties

Of natural

Delightful flair

Of bondage in wear that can appear

To be a custom lens of a being

Lifted upright through strength

Head held high with strife

No suddenness of fear but fury

The wrath to overcome and be

The women that God wants you to see

Built in your own right

Despite the raw material that overflows

Outshines the wisdom and worth that holds

* * *

I am an African American woman. And I love to uplift my beautiful black queens. That is definitely what I did. It is very necessary to do so because it can be lacking in many areas. We are powerful beings who really do not get the credit where it is due. This poem showcases black women for who they are. From my lenses it's art that I want to share. You're welcome.

Reflection

_____

_____

_____

_____

_____

_____

_____

_____

_____

_____

_____

_____

_____

_____

_____

_____

_____

_____

_____

_____

_____

_____

_____

A Quiet Song

A mist off in the distance

The breeze coasting against my face

Appears to be a delight song

The rhythm of streams

Acquaints my ears with a certain pace

Smooth vibrations

Along the whistles of thy breath

It's gentle to the touch

Mythical as such

The connected waves of sound

Open for rooms of silence

The eloquence

Of symmetrical elegance

Sways

Glides

Arrives

With the music of sound

So beautiful in tone

* * *

Have you ever listened to music and really just listened? Music is medicine to my ears. It puts me in a place where I'm very relaxed and just in tune, muting the outside world. It may be loud but can be very much quiet. Do you agree?

Reflection

_____

_____

_____

_____

_____

_____

_____

_____

_____

_____

_____

_____

_____

_____

_____

_____

_____

_____

_____

_____

_____

_____

_____

The Gentleman

Courtesy so gentle

Poise that is imposed

Comes across wholehearted

Smoothly conniving

Effortlessly thriving

Visionary of the finest

Lady magnet among the realest

Provides a sense of security

Provides a sense of fidelity

Underlying the naughty consciousness

Of devouring the soul

A sexual intention in making you whole

It reveals

Tempted feels

Your undivided attention

Of unnoticed appreciation

He is known

To be

The Gentleman

* * *

Every woman may seek a gentle man, described as such. There are many within our society, waiting to be noticed. Have you met your gentleman? Or yet are you that gentleman?

Reflection

_____

_____

_____

_____

_____

_____

_____

_____

_____

_____

_____

_____

_____

_____

_____

_____

_____

_____

_____

_____

_____

Red...Black...White

The Red I see

So pure and bright

As bloody as an orange

But strong as the soul

It carries truth that never lies

Holds belief in disguise

When I am wrong and when I am right

The discussion rolls and plays out

The Black I see

So rich and loving

Sense of laughter omits

The true being of realness commits

This has interlinked the two solely

Close-knit figures

Brings nothing but joy fully

The White I see

A flash of awe

Who knew this would come forth?

Passionate understanding of thought

Outlays the sensitivity of mind

Senses of what was shared have brought

Undivided attention that was never oversought

Red Black and White

* * *

As you can see, the three signify some sort of meaning. As stated in a previous poem, colors are so much more than coloring or a splotch of something on a canvas. They circulate attributes that are of value to someone to share the truth of feelings for another. Rather than stating the obvious, why not elaborate on each color that kind of depicts a person apart? It's very interesting and can put a unique spin on things.

Reflection

_____

_____

_____

_____

_____

_____

_____

_____

_____

_____

_____

_____

_____

_____

_____

_____

_____

_____

_____

_____

_____

_____

_____

_____

_____

_____

Element

What do you think?
That drive that keeps you going
What do you feel?
The antics of energized mimics
The pressure
Very much so de-escalating
The tension of leisure
Foot on the petal
Slow…steady…squeeze
The anticipation evaluates itself
The understanding guides itself
The concentration focuses itself
The "in to win"
The "I can't "
No excuse of interpretation
To disclose your utter fascination
Of "I'm going to do"
Vs.
"Doing it"
Vision of a go-getter
Holds the tongue
Of a nonbeliever
Of a quitter
Bottom-feeder
A non-having ass achiever

The pointless response

That cannot be driven away

Hold it

Throw it

Belittle it

The control is overdue

The element that

you cherish

Is flourish

It is yours

You are in it

Your element

* * *

The moment of your awakening, overseeing all the negative and derogatory slander. You are your own drive toward succeeding in what it is you believe and strive for. No one can take that away from you. As long as you believe in it, nothing else matters. Your element keeps you focused, balanced, and controlled within your own mental and physical capacity.

Reflection

_____
_____
_____
_____
_____
_____
_____
_____
_____
_____
_____
_____
_____
_____
_____
_____
_____
_____
_____
_____
_____
_____
_____

The Cry

Off in the distance

Sweeps the cold winds away

The melting of the snow

The fireflies brighten with a shiny glow

The mixing of the seasons

Enhances streams of lenses

Shallow up in one sitting

Allows overflowing emotions

Of this fine beginning

An aura that is held at might

The strong will held in through the night

It's stumbles

Hardly fumbles

The drops on a dreary morning

Drowsy eyes slowly forming

A weakness from within

Pours out a cry of today's end

* * *

Crying can be for any reason. It could be from stress. It can be from pain. It can be from joy and just simple happiness. What is your cry?

Reflection

_____

_____

_____

_____

_____

_____

_____

_____

_____

_____

_____

_____

_____

_____

_____

_____

_____

_____

_____

_____

_____

_____

Beautiful

It is
Light
Presence
Everything connected
Disconnected
Darkness
Glistens
Shining
Doors
Being open
Good
Bad
Ugly
Personality
Wavering
In and out
Thoughts lingering
Ups
Downs
Testaments
Battles
Won
Loss
It is
Who we are
What we are

What we do

What we see

What we think

Optimistic

Mind

Open

Closed

Everything

We touch

We believe

What is wrong

What is right

A choice

A decision

It is

Beautiful

No matter what

The world is made up

Likes

Dislikes

Love

Hate

It is

What makes it

Beautiful

* * *

What we call beautiful has many imperfections. They may cause triggers or senses of depression. Something so beautiful can be so numb. It's quite mind-boggling, but it's meant to be. For example, the beautiful thing about individuals living within society is literally "living." Yes, we go through battles that may cause us to think negatively on many matters, but that comes and goes. At the end of the day, what we face shapes who we are, and in all reality that is a beautiful thing. What do you think?

Reflection

_____

_____

_____

_____

_____

_____

_____

_____

_____

_____

_____

_____

_____

_____

_____

_____

_____

_____

_____

_____

_____

Butterflies

Eyes glistening

Heart beating

Smiles arise from miles away

Sensing the nerves seeping over me

The feeling

It's full of ecstasy

That shall not pass

I have this

For you

* * *

Those fluttering feelings you feel in the pit of your stomach. The name that pops up on a message, the first look when you see that certain individual, the antsy feeling when you are patiently but impatiently awaiting a response from someone you really have something for. It's quite an intense feeling that does not ever want to end. That right there is called butterflies.

Reflection

_____
_____
_____
_____
_____
_____
_____
_____
_____
_____
_____
_____
_____
_____
_____
_____
_____
_____
_____
_____
_____
_____

CPSIA information can be obtained
at www.ICGtesting.com
Printed in the USA
LVHW021615270422
717239LV00014B/1340

9 781685 151386